WHAT IS
FRACTIONAL HR?

Crystal Coast HR

DAVID M ARNOLD, MS, SPHR

This Page is Blank

Disclaimer

The information provided in this eBook is for educational and informational purposes only. While every effort has been made to ensure the accuracy and reliability of the content, the author and publisher make no representations or warranties of any kind, express or implied, about the completeness, accuracy, reliability, or suitability of the information provided. The use of the information in this eBook is at the reader's own risk.

The content within this eBook is not intended to serve as legal, financial, or professional advice. Business owners, HR managers, and entrepreneurs should consult with qualified professionals—such as legal advisors, accountants, or certified HR experts—before making any decisions regarding their HR practices, policies, or strategies.

The application of Fractional HR and its benefits may vary depending on the unique circumstances and requirements of each business. The author and publisher are not responsible for any actions taken based on the information in this eBook or any consequences that may arise from its use.

By reading this eBook, you agree to hold the author and publisher harmless from any liabilities or damages that may occur as a result of relying on the content provided. Always conduct your own research and seek advice from relevant experts when making decisions that impact your business or HR practices.

This eBook may contain links to third-party websites or resources. These links are provided for convenience, and the author does not endorse or take responsibility for the content of any external sites.

Copyright Notice

Table of Contents

Preface

In the ever-evolving landscape of business, human resources (HR) plays a pivotal role in driving success. From recruiting the right talent to fostering a positive work environment, HR is at the heart of any organization's ability to thrive. However, for many small to medium-sized enterprises (SMEs), maintaining a robust HR function can be a daunting task. The costs associated with hiring full-time HR professionals, coupled with the time and resources required to manage an in-house team, often present significant challenges.

Enter Fractional HR—a flexible, cost-effective solution that allows businesses to tap into the expertise of seasoned HR professionals without the financial burden of a full-time HR department. This model has gained traction in recent years, offering businesses of all sizes the ability to access HR expertise on a part-time or project-based basis. Whether you're a startup looking to scale quickly, an established business in need of specialized HR support, or a growing company navigating complex employee issues, Fractional HR provides the tools and resources to address your unique challenges.

This eBook was created to help demystify Fractional HR and explore how this innovative model can transform your approach to human resources. As a business owner, HR manager, or entrepreneur, you are constantly juggling multiple priorities. The last thing you want is to be bogged down by HR tasks that don't align with your core business goals. Fractional HR gives you the flexibility to delegate these responsibilities to professionals who can manage them efficiently, allowing you to focus on what matters most—growing your business.

Throughout the chapters, we'll dive into the fundamentals of Fractional HR, how it works, the key areas where it adds value, and how you can select the right HR partner for your needs. You will gain a clear understanding of how Fractional HR can help streamline your operations, save costs, enhance employee engagement, and ensure compliance with ever-changing regulations. From recruitment and compliance to performance management and employee retention, Fractional HR provides a strategic approach to HR management that is tailored to your organization's goals and resources.

Whether you are new to the concept of Fractional HR or looking for ways to optimize an existing HR function, this guide will provide you with the knowledge and insights necessary to make informed decisions. By the end of this eBook, you will have a clear understanding of how Fractional HR can benefit your business, helping you unlock the full potential of your human capital.

As you read, consider how the principles and strategies outlined here can be applied to your organization. The world of work is changing rapidly, and with the right HR support, you can position your business for success in an increasingly competitive environment. Let's explore how Fractional HR can be the key to unlocking your business's potential.

Introduction

In today's rapidly evolving business landscape, managing human resources (HR) effectively is no longer a luxury but a necessity. However, for many small to medium-sized enterprises (SMEs), establishing and maintaining a full-fledged HR department can be financially prohibitive. At the same time, failing to address HR needs adequately can lead to inefficiencies, compliance risks, and decreased employee satisfaction. This is where Fractional HR comes into play—offering businesses the flexibility and expertise of a professional HR function without the overhead costs of full-time employees.

Purpose of the eBook

The purpose of this eBook is to provide a comprehensive guide to Fractional HR services, illustrating how they can help modern businesses thrive. As an alternative to traditional, full-time HR models, Fractional HR allows businesses to access expert-level HR support on a part-time or project basis, making it an ideal solution for small and mid-sized companies. This eBook explores the key benefits, challenges, and practical steps associated with adopting Fractional HR, and how businesses can leverage this model to scale operations, enhance employee engagement, improve compliance, and reduce overall costs.

In today's dynamic work environment, HR functions are more critical than ever, touching everything from recruitment and performance management to employee engagement and legal compliance. Understanding how Fractional HR can be seamlessly integrated into your business structure is vital for keeping pace with changes in workforce needs, technological advancements, and regulatory requirements. Whether you are just beginning to think about your company's HR strategy or are looking for a more flexible, cost-effective HR solution, this eBook will help you navigate the world of Fractional HR with confidence and insight.

Definition of Fractional HR

Fractional HR refers to a flexible, outsourced model where businesses contract part-time or project-based HR services, rather than hiring a full-time HR team. In essence, businesses can access specialized HR expertise on an as-needed basis, tailoring their HR support to the specific needs of the organization. This model allows small to medium-sized enterprises to benefit from professional HR management without the significant financial investment of a full-time in-house HR department.

The term "fractional" refers to the fact that businesses are not paying for a full-time employee but rather are hiring HR professionals to fulfill specific functions or tasks at a reduced scale. These services can be limited to one particular HR function, such as recruitment or compliance, or more comprehensive, covering a range of HR responsibilities like performance management, employee training, and compensation analysis. The flexibility inherent in the Fractional HR model allows businesses to scale up or down based on changing HR needs and budget constraints.

Fractional HR is distinctly different from traditional HR models in several key ways:

- **Cost Efficiency:** Traditional HR departments require full-time staff, which incurs not only salaries but also benefits, office space, and additional overhead costs. Fractional HR eliminates these expenses by allowing businesses to access HR expertise on a part-time basis.

- **Flexibility:** Fractional HR providers can be engaged for a specific duration or project, and services can be adjusted as needs evolve. This flexibility allows businesses to address immediate challenges like recruiting, compliance audits, or employee training without long-term commitments.

- **Expertise on Demand:** With Fractional HR, businesses gain access to a higher level of HR expertise than they may be able to afford with a full-time in-house team. These professionals bring a wealth of experience across various industries, allowing them to implement best practices that drive organizational success.

Overall, Fractional HR offers a customized approach to managing human resources, providing businesses with the ability to tackle HR challenges efficiently and effectively without overextending resources.

Target Audience

This eBook is aimed at business owners, HR managers, and entrepreneurs—particularly those working in small to medium-sized enterprises (SMEs)—who are seeking to optimize their HR functions. Whether you're a startup looking to establish an HR framework, a growing business needing more advanced HR services, or an established company wanting to improve operational efficiency, this guide will provide valuable insights into leveraging Fractional HR as a strategic tool.

For small and mid-sized businesses that don't have the resources for a full-time HR department, Fractional HR can be a game-changer. This model allows them to access specialized HR services without the financial burden associated with a dedicated in-house team. As HR management becomes increasingly complex with changing regulations, diversity initiatives, and evolving workplace trends, Fractional HR helps businesses stay compliant and competitive while keeping costs manageable.

Moreover, entrepreneurs who are scaling their businesses may find that Fractional HR provides the flexibility they need to address the changing demands of their workforce without getting bogged down by administrative tasks. Fractional

HR allows leaders to focus on growing their business, knowing that their HR needs are in capable hands.

Ultimately, this eBook is for those looking to optimize their business operations through smarter HR solutions—whether you're looking to streamline recruiting, improve employee engagement, ensure compliance, or boost overall organizational performance. By understanding the potential of Fractional HR, you can make informed decisions that align with your company's strategic goals.

In the following chapters, we will explore the fundamentals of Fractional HR, the benefits it offers, how to choose the right HR partner, and much more. Let's dive deeper into this cost-effective and flexible approach to HR management and discover how it can benefit your business today.

Chapter 1:

Understanding Fractional HR

1.1 What Is Fractional HR?

Definition and Explanation of the Concept

Fractional HR refers to the practice of hiring experienced Human Resources (HR) professionals on a part-time or as-needed basis, rather than employing a full-time HR staff. This flexible model allows businesses to access a high level of HR expertise without the commitment and expense of a full-time hire. The term "fractional" emphasizes that businesses are only engaging a fraction of the HR professional's time, allowing them to pay for exactly what they need.

Unlike traditional HR roles, which might require a full-time commitment with benefits and other associated costs, fractional HR professionals offer their services for a set number of hours per week or month, or on a project-by-project basis. They handle a range of HR tasks, from recruitment and employee onboarding to compliance, employee relations, and performance management. This model is ideal for businesses that need professional HR support but do not require a full-time HR department.

Fractional HR is gaining traction in the modern workforce due to its flexibility, cost-effectiveness, and scalability. It aligns with the broader trend of fractional work, which includes fractional CFOs, CMOs, and other executive roles that allow companies to tap into high-level expertise without incurring the full-time costs.

Origins of Fractional HR and Its Rise in Popularity

The concept of fractional HR has its roots in the growing demand for more flexible and cost-effective business solutions. As companies began to recognize that their HR needs varied throughout the year—sometimes needing intensive support during periods of growth or organizational change, and less during stable times—the demand for a scalable HR solution became apparent.

The rise of the gig economy and remote work culture further accelerated the adoption of fractional HR. As more professionals began offering their skills on a freelance or contract basis, businesses found it easier to access specialized talent without geographical limitations. Fractional HR became particularly appealing during economic downturns or uncertain times, such as during the COVID-19 pandemic, when businesses needed to streamline operations, reduce costs, and remain agile.

The shift towards a more dynamic, project-based workforce model has allowed businesses to adapt quickly to changing market conditions. Fractional HR has emerged as a strategic solution, enabling companies to maintain HR compliance, enhance employee engagement, and manage their workforce more efficiently, all while keeping operational costs under control.

Comparison with Traditional In-House HR and HR Outsourcing

To fully understand the value of fractional HR, it's essential to compare it with traditional in-house HR and HR outsourcing:

Traditional In-House HR:

This model involves hiring full-time HR staff who are fully integrated into the company. They handle everything from payroll and compliance to employee development and strategic HR initiatives. While this approach ensures that HR is always available, it comes with significant costs, including salaries, benefits, and overhead. Additionally, in-house HR teams may not always have the specialized skills required for every HR challenge.

HR Outsourcing:

Outsourcing HR involves delegating HR functions to an external agency. This can include payroll processing, benefits administration, recruitment, and compliance management. While HR outsourcing can reduce the administrative burden, it often lacks the personalized touch and deep understanding of the company's culture and needs. Outsourcing can also be less flexible, as contracts with HR service providers may be rigid, making it challenging to adapt to changing business requirements.

Fractional HR:

Fractional HR offers the best of both worlds. It provides access to experienced HR professionals who can work on-site or remotely, as needed. Unlike traditional outsourcing, fractional HR specialists become a part of your team, albeit on a part-time basis, ensuring a more tailored and personalized approach. This model is particularly advantageous for small to mid-sized businesses that need specialized HR support without the financial burden of a full-time hire.

1.2 Key Benefits of Fractional HR

Cost Efficiency and Flexibility

One of the most significant advantages of fractional HR is its cost efficiency. Hiring full-time HR staff can be expensive, especially for small businesses that may not have the budget for additional salaries, benefits, and other associated costs. Fractional HR provides a more affordable alternative by allowing businesses to pay only for the services they need. This can include a set number of hours per week or month, or project-based engagements, such as handling a recruitment drive or setting up a new performance management system.

Flexibility is another critical benefit of fractional HR. Businesses can adjust the level of HR support based on their current needs, whether it's scaling up during periods of rapid growth or scaling down during slower times. This flexibility helps businesses remain agile, enabling them to respond quickly to changes in the market or internal challenges.

Access to Experienced HR Professionals on a Part-Time Basis

With fractional HR, companies gain access to seasoned HR professionals who bring years of experience to the table. These professionals often have a diverse background, having worked across multiple industries and business sizes. This broad experience allows them to provide strategic insights and innovative solutions that can enhance HR operations.

For startups and small businesses, this access to high-level HR expertise can be invaluable. It enables them to implement best practices from day one, helping them avoid costly mistakes and ensuring compliance with labor laws and regulations. For larger companies, fractional HR professionals can supplement the existing HR team, offering specialized skills that may be lacking in-house.

Scalability to Meet the Changing Needs of a Growing Business

As businesses grow, their HR needs become more complex. What started as a few employees managed by a single office manager can quickly evolve into a full-fledged HR operation requiring specialized knowledge in areas such as compliance, employee engagement, and performance management.

Fractional HR offers the scalability needed to support this growth. Companies can start with a fractional HR professional handling basic HR tasks and gradually increase their involvement as the business expands. This model is especially beneficial for companies in growth phases, mergers and acquisitions, or undergoing significant organizational changes.

Increased Focus on Core Business Functions by Delegating HR Responsibilities

Managing HR internally can be time-consuming and distracting, especially for business owners and managers who are not HR experts. By outsourcing HR functions to a fractional HR professional, businesses can free up their time and resources to focus on core business activities, such as sales, marketing, and product development.

Fractional HR can take care of everything from compliance and benefits administration to employee relations and performance management, allowing companies to operate more efficiently. This delegation of HR responsibilities not only reduces the administrative burden but also improves the overall productivity and profitability of the business.

1.3 Who Can Benefit from Fractional HR?

Startups and Small Businesses with Limited HR Budgets

Startups and small businesses often operate on tight budgets, making it challenging to hire full-time HR staff. Fractional HR offers an affordable solution that enables these businesses to access professional HR support without the high costs associated with full-time hires.

For startups, getting HR right from the beginning is crucial. Fractional HR can help establish essential HR processes, such as hiring, onboarding, compliance, and performance management, which sets the foundation for future growth. By leveraging fractional HR, small businesses can remain compliant, reduce legal risks, and foster a positive work environment, all of which are vital for attracting and retaining talent.

Mid-Sized Companies Looking to Optimize HR Operations

Mid-sized companies often have more established HR needs but may not require a full-time HR team for every function. Fractional HR can supplement existing HR staff, providing expertise in areas like compliance audits, employee training, leadership development, and strategic planning.

This model allows mid-sized companies to optimize their HR operations by focusing on specific areas of improvement. For example, a fractional HR professional can help with the implementation of new HR software, design a robust employee engagement program, or lead a diversity and inclusion initiative. By bringing in a fractional HR expert, mid-sized businesses can achieve their HR goals more efficiently and effectively.

Organizations Undergoing Change or Growth Phases

Organizations undergoing significant changes, such as mergers, acquisitions, or rapid expansion, often face complex HR challenges. Fractional HR can provide the strategic support needed during these transitions, ensuring that HR processes are aligned with the company's new direction.

For instance, during a merger, a fractional HR professional can assist with integrating employee policies, managing communication with staff, and aligning the corporate culture of the merging entities. Similarly, during periods of rapid growth, fractional HR can help scale recruitment efforts, implement training programs, and establish robust performance management systems to support the expanding workforce.

Fractional HR also plays a vital role in change management by helping organizations navigate the complexities of restructuring, downsizing, or shifting business strategies. By providing on-demand HR expertise, fractional HR professionals enable companies to adapt to change with minimal disruption to their operations.

Conclusion of Chapter 1

Understanding the concept of fractional HR is crucial for businesses looking to optimize their HR functions while maintaining flexibility and cost efficiency. Whether you are a startup needing foundational HR support, a mid-sized company looking to optimize specific areas, or an organization navigating change, fractional HR offers a scalable solution that aligns with your business needs. In the next chapter, we will explore how fractional HR works in practice, including the different engagement models and best practices for implementation.

Chapter 2:

How Fractional HR Works

2.1 The Role of a Fractional HR Manager

Fractional HR has become an increasingly popular solution for companies seeking to streamline their HR functions without the cost burden of a full-time HR department. At the core of this model is the **Fractional HR Manager**, who brings specialized expertise to handle various HR tasks on a flexible, part-time basis.

Typical Responsibilities

The responsibilities of a Fractional HR Manager can vary widely depending on the needs of the organization. However, their role typically encompasses the following areas:

Recruitment and Talent Acquisition:

One of the primary tasks of a Fractional HR Manager is managing the recruitment process. This can include everything from crafting job descriptions, posting job ads, screening resumes, conducting interviews, and negotiating job offers. They ensure that the hiring process aligns with the company's goals and culture while also helping to source the best talent for each role.

Compliance and Legal Issues:

Ensuring compliance with labor laws and regulations is crucial for any business, especially in highly regulated industries. Fractional HR Managers stay up-to-date with the latest HR laws and can help organizations navigate complex regulations such as the Family and Medical Leave Act (FMLA), Occupational Safety and Health Administration (OSHA) standards, and Equal Employment Opportunity

(EEO) laws. By managing compliance, they reduce the risk of legal issues and penalties.

Employee Relations:

Maintaining a positive work environment is essential for employee satisfaction and retention. Fractional HR Managers are skilled in handling employee relations, addressing workplace conflicts, conducting investigations into complaints, and fostering open communication channels between employees and management. This support is especially beneficial for small businesses that may not have an internal HR team to mediate sensitive issues.

Benefits Administration:

Another critical area of focus is benefits administration. Fractional HR Managers can manage employee benefits programs, including health insurance, retirement plans, and other perks. They help businesses design competitive benefits packages that attract and retain talent while staying within budget. They can also handle the annual open enrollment process, ensuring employees understand their options and can make informed decisions.

Performance Management and Employee Development:

Fractional HR Managers play a vital role in developing performance management systems, conducting employee reviews, and providing feedback to foster growth and improvement. They may implement training programs, develop career progression paths, and design employee engagement initiatives to boost morale and productivity.

Policy Development and HR Strategy:

Beyond the day-to-day HR tasks, Fractional HR Managers are strategic partners. They can assist in developing HR policies, creating employee handbooks, and setting up HR frameworks that align with the company's overall business strategy. By leveraging their expertise, businesses can build a strong foundation for their workforce.

The Difference Between a Fractional HR Manager and a Traditional HR Manager

While both Fractional HR Managers and traditional HR Managers perform similar functions, the key difference lies in their engagement model and cost structure:

- **Flexibility**: Fractional HR Managers offer greater flexibility as they work on a part-time or project basis. This allows businesses to scale HR support up or down based on their current needs, making it an ideal solution for companies experiencing fluctuations in workload or undergoing changes.

- **Cost-Effectiveness**: Hiring a full-time HR Manager comes with a significant financial commitment, including salary, benefits, and overhead costs. Fractional HR Managers, on the other hand, are typically paid only for the hours they work or the specific projects they complete. This results in considerable cost savings, particularly for small to mid-sized businesses.

- **Specialized Expertise**: Fractional HR Managers often bring a wealth of experience across various industries and business sizes.

This enables them to provide strategic insights and best practices that a traditional HR Manager with limited experience may not have. Companies benefit from high-level HR expertise without the need to invest in long-term employment contracts.

2.2 Models of Engagement

Fractional HR services are highly adaptable, offering different engagement models to suit the unique needs of each business. Understanding these models can help organizations choose the right approach for their HR requirements.

Retainer-Based Models

In a **retainer-based model**, businesses engage a Fractional HR Manager for a set number of hours per week or month. This model is ideal for companies that require consistent HR support but do not need a full-time HR professional. The retainer ensures that the HR Manager is available to handle ongoing tasks, such as employee relations, compliance, and payroll support.

Benefits of the Retainer Model:

- **Predictable Costs**: Businesses pay a fixed fee for a set number of hours, making budgeting easier.

- **Consistent Support**: Provides ongoing access to HR expertise, which is beneficial for handling regular HR functions.

- **Relationship Building**: Over time, the Fractional HR Manager becomes familiar with the company's culture, enabling them to provide more tailored advice.

Best For:

- Growing businesses that need steady HR support.

- Companies with recurring HR needs, such as regular hiring or employee performance reviews.

Project-Based Models

The **project-based model** is suited for businesses that require HR expertise for a specific project or initiative. Examples include setting up an HR department, conducting an employee engagement survey, implementing a new HR software system, or managing a major recruitment drive.

Benefits of the Project-Based Model:

- **Flexibility**: Businesses only pay for the duration of the project, making it a cost-effective solution for short-term needs.

- **Specialized Expertise**: Allows access to HR professionals with specialized skills relevant to the project.

- **Clear Scope and Deliverables**: Projects typically have defined objectives, timelines, and outcomes, ensuring clarity and accountability.

Best For:

- Startups needing help with initial HR setup.

- Companies undergoing mergers, acquisitions, or organizational changes.

- Organizations looking to implement new HR technologies or policies.

On-Demand HR Support

The **on-demand model** offers the most flexibility, allowing businesses to engage HR professionals only when needed. This could include situations such as handling a complex employee relations issue, conducting compliance audits, or providing interim HR leadership during a transition.

Benefits of the On-Demand Model:

- **Ultimate Flexibility**: Pay-as-you-go structure ensures that businesses only pay for what they need, when they need it.

- **Rapid Response**: Ideal for urgent or unexpected HR issues that require immediate attention.

- **Cost Control**: No long-term commitment, making it the most flexible and cost-efficient option.

Best For:

- Small businesses with occasional HR needs.

- Companies facing unexpected HR challenges, like handling layoffs or addressing compliance breaches.

- Organizations needing temporary HR leadership during a vacancy.

2.3 How to Implement Fractional HR

Successfully implementing a fractional HR model requires careful planning and consideration. Here are the steps to ensure a smooth transition and effective use of fractional HR services.

Assessing Your Organization's HR Needs

Before engaging a Fractional HR professional, it's crucial to assess your current HR needs and challenges. This involves:

- **Conducting an HR Audit**: Evaluate your existing HR processes, policies, and compliance status. Identify gaps and areas for improvement.

- **Determining the Scope of Work**: Define what HR functions you need support with. Are you looking for help with recruitment, compliance, employee relations, or strategic HR planning?

- **Estimating the Time Commitment**: Assess whether your needs are ongoing (suitable for a retainer model), project-based, or occasional (ideal for on-demand support).

This assessment will help you determine the right level of HR support required and select the most appropriate engagement model.

Choosing the Right Fractional HR Provider

Selecting the right Fractional HR provider is essential for achieving your HR goals. Here's what to consider during the selection process:

- **Experience and Expertise**: Look for HR professionals with experience relevant to your industry and business size. Review their credentials, past projects, and client testimonials.

- **Flexibility and Availability**: Ensure that the provider can accommodate your preferred engagement model, whether it's retainer-based, project-based, or on-demand.

- **Cultural Fit**: Since HR involves managing sensitive aspects of your workforce, it's important that the Fractional HR Manager aligns with your company's values and culture.

- **Communication Skills:** Effective communication is key to a successful partnership. Choose an HR provider who is responsive, proactive, and transparent in their communication.

Conduct interviews and request proposals from multiple providers to compare their services, pricing, and approach before making your decision.

Setting Clear Expectations and Deliverables

To maximize the value of fractional HR services, it's crucial to establish clear expectations and deliverables from the outset. This involves:

- **Defining Goals and Objectives:** Clearly articulate what you aim to achieve through fractional HR support, such as improving employee retention, ensuring compliance, or streamlining recruitment processes.

- **Creating a Service Agreement:** Develop a detailed agreement that outlines the scope of work, engagement model, expected deliverables, timelines, and pricing. This serves as a reference point to avoid misunderstandings.

- **Regular Check-Ins and Performance Reviews**: Schedule regular check-ins to assess progress, provide feedback, and make adjustments as needed. This helps ensure that the fractional HR services are aligned with your evolving business needs.

By taking these steps, you can establish a productive partnership with your Fractional HR Manager, ensuring that they deliver value to your organization.

Conclusion of Chapter 2

Fractional HR offers a flexible and cost-effective solution for businesses looking to enhance their HR capabilities without the overhead of full-time staff. By understanding the role of a Fractional HR Manager, exploring the different models of engagement, and implementing best practices, businesses can leverage fractional HR to optimize their workforce management, stay compliant, and drive growth.

In the next chapter, we will dive into real-world case studies showcasing the impact of fractional HR on various businesses, highlighting the tangible benefits and lessons learned from their experiences.

Chapter 3:

Key Areas Where Fractional HR Adds Value

Fractional HR is more than just a cost-effective alternative to traditional HR models—it is a strategic approach that empowers organizations to optimize their human resources functions. In this chapter, we explore the key areas where Fractional HR can significantly add value to businesses, helping them streamline operations, enhance compliance, and foster a positive workplace culture.

3.1 Recruitment & Staffing

Recruitment is one of the most critical HR functions, as hiring the right talent can make or break a business. However, many companies, especially small to mid-sized organizations, struggle with the complexities of the hiring process. This is where Fractional HR can provide substantial support.

How Fractional HR Can Streamline Hiring Processes

Fractional HR professionals bring extensive experience in recruitment strategies, making them adept at optimizing the hiring process. They can:

- **Craft Tailored Job Descriptions**: By understanding the specific needs of your business, Fractional HR experts can create job descriptions that attract qualified candidates. They know how to highlight key skills and responsibilities to draw in the right talent.

- **Implement Efficient Recruitment Strategies**: Fractional HR can streamline your hiring pipeline by leveraging best practices, including using Applicant Tracking

Systems (ATS) and optimizing job postings for online platforms like LinkedIn, Indeed, and Glassdoor.

- **Reduce Time-to-Hire**: With their experience
- can quickly source, screen, and shortlist candidates, significantly reducing the time it takes to fill open positions.

Interviewing, Onboarding, and Training Support

Beyond sourcing candidates, Fractional HR Managers can also manage the interview process, onboarding, and initial training:

- **Structured Interview Processes**: They design structured interview formats that assess candidates' competencies, cultural fit, and potential to contribute to the company's growth. This helps reduce bias and improve the quality of hires.

- **Effective Onboarding Programs**: A strong onboarding process is crucial for employee retention. Fractional HR Managers develop onboarding programs that ensure new hires are integrated into the company culture, understand their roles, and are set up for success from day one.

- **Training and Development Support**: New employees often require training to get up to speed. Fractional HR can design training modules tailored to specific roles, ensuring that new hires are productive quickly.

3.2 Compliance & Risk Management

Compliance with labor laws and industry regulations is a major concern for businesses, especially as the legal landscape continues to evolve. Failure to comply can result in hefty fines, lawsuits, and reputational damage. Fractional HR experts help mitigate these risks.

Ensuring Compliance with Labor Laws and Regulations

Fractional HR professionals stay up-to-date with the latest labor laws and regulations, ensuring that your business remains compliant. They can:

- **Audit HR Policies**: Conduct audits of existing HR policies to identify gaps or areas that require updates. This includes reviewing employee handbooks, contracts, and other legal documents.

- **Update Workplace Policies**: Implementing clear and compliant workplace policies is essential for avoiding legal disputes. Fractional HR Managers can help develop or update policies related to equal employment opportunity (EEO), harassment, and workplace safety.

Implementing Workplace Policies and Procedures

Fractional HR can help you establish a framework of policies and procedures that align with your business objectives:

- **Creating Employee Handbooks**: They develop comprehensive employee handbooks that outline company policies, procedures, and expectations, ensuring all employees are aware of their rights and responsibilities.

- **Developing Code of Conduct**: Fractional HR Managers can implement a code of conduct to establish ethical guidelines for behavior in the workplace, which is crucial for maintaining a positive work environment.

Handling Sensitive Employee Issues and Investigations

Workplace conflicts, complaints, or allegations of misconduct can disrupt business operations. Fractional HR professionals are skilled at managing these sensitive situations:

- **Conducting Investigations**: They can handle internal investigations with discretion, ensuring fairness and compliance with legal standards.

- **Mediating Disputes**: Fractional HR Managers can act as impartial mediators to resolve employee disputes and foster a collaborative work environment.

3.3 Performance Management

Effective performance management is crucial for driving employee productivity and achieving business goals. Fractional HR professionals bring expertise in designing systems that motivate and engage employees.

Designing and Implementing Performance Review Systems

Fractional HR Managers can help you establish performance management systems that drive results:

- **Developing Review Frameworks**: They design performance review frameworks that align with your business objectives, incorporating self-assessments, peer reviews, and management evaluations.

- **Conducting Appraisals**: Fractional HR can facilitate regular performance appraisals, providing objective feedback and setting development goals for employees.

Coaching and Development Plans for Employees

To foster employee growth, Fractional HR experts can implement personalized coaching and development plans:

- **Career Development**: They create career progression paths to help employees understand their growth potential within the company.

- **Skill Enhancement**: They identify skill gaps and recommend training programs to enhance employee capabilities, thereby boosting job satisfaction and retention.

Setting Up Key Performance Indicators (KPIs)

Fractional HR Managers can help businesses set up KPIs that align with strategic goals:

- **Measurable Metrics**: Establishing KPIs allows for the measurement of employee performance against specific goals, helping managers identify high performers and areas for improvement.

- **Regular Feedback**: By setting up regular feedback loops, Fractional HR ensures that employees are continuously aligned with organizational objectives.

3.4 Compensation & Benefits

A competitive compensation package is essential for attracting and retaining top talent. Fractional HR experts provide valuable insights into designing pay structures and benefits programs that align with market trends.

Developing Competitive Compensation Packages

Fractional HR professionals conduct market research to develop competitive compensation strategies:

- **Salary Benchmarking**: They analyze industry standards to ensure that your pay scales are competitive, helping to attract high-caliber talent.

- **Incentive Plans**: Fractional HR Managers can design bonus structures, commission plans, and other incentive programs to motivate employees.

Managing Employee Benefits and Perks

An attractive benefits package goes beyond just salary:

- **Health and Wellness Programs**: Fractional HR experts can design health, dental, and vision insurance plans, along with wellness programs that support employee well-being.

- **Retirement Plans**: They assist in setting up 401(k) plans, pensions, and other retirement benefits, ensuring compliance with financial regulations.

Advising on Payroll and Compensation Compliance

Ensuring compliance with payroll regulations is crucial to avoid penalties:

- **Fair Labor Standards Act (FLSA) Compliance**: Fractional HR can audit your payroll processes to ensure compliance with overtime pay, minimum wage, and other FLSA requirements.

- **Equity and Transparency**: They advise on pay equity to eliminate disparities and foster a fair workplace.

3.5 Employee Engagement & Retention

Employee engagement is a key driver of productivity and retention. Fractional HR professionals implement strategies that create a positive and engaging work environment.

Strategies to Improve Employee Morale and Engagement

Fractional HR Managers can design initiatives to boost employee morale:

- **Recognition Programs**: Implementing recognition programs to celebrate employee achievements, which can significantly increase job satisfaction.

- **Team-Building Activities**: Organizing team-building exercises and events to foster collaboration and camaraderie.

Conducting Employee Surveys and Feedback Sessions

Regular feedback is vital for continuous improvement:

- **Pulse Surveys**: Fractional HR can conduct pulse surveys to gauge employee satisfaction and identify areas for improvement.

- **Focus Groups**: They facilitate focus groups and feedback sessions to understand employee concerns and gather suggestions.

Designing Employee Recognition Programs

Recognition is a powerful motivator:

- **Rewards Systems**: Creating reward systems that align with company values, such as employee of the month awards, spot bonuses, and other incentives.

- **Career Milestone Celebrations**: Recognizing employee anniversaries, promotions, and achievements to foster loyalty.

3.6 Training & Development

Investing in training and development is essential for building a skilled workforce. Fractional HR can help create and implement effective training programs.

Creating and Delivering Training Programs

Fractional HR professionals can design customized training programs:

- **New Hire Training**: They develop onboarding training that helps new employees acclimate quickly and effectively.

- **Skill Development Workshops**: Designing workshops focused on specific skills like communication, leadership, or technical abilities.

Leadership Development and Succession Planning

To ensure future leadership, Fractional HR Managers can:

- **Identify High Potentials**: Implement leadership development programs aimed at grooming high-potential employees for future management roles.

- **Succession Planning**: Create succession plans to prepare for critical role transitions, reducing the impact of key employee departures.

Upskilling and Reskilling Initiatives

The rapid pace of technological change requires continuous learning:

- **Continuous Learning Programs**: They implement programs to upskill and reskill employees, ensuring that your workforce remains competitive.

- **eLearning Platforms**: Fractional HR can integrate online learning platforms and resources to facilitate continuous professional development.

Conclusion of Chapter 3

Fractional HR provides invaluable support across a range of critical HR functions, from recruitment to compliance, performance management, and employee engagement. By leveraging the expertise of Fractional HR professionals, organizations can optimize their HR processes, improve employee satisfaction, and drive sustainable growth.

In the next chapter, we will explore **real-world case studies** to demonstrate how Fractional HR has made a tangible impact on businesses of different sizes and industries. These case studies will highlight the versatility and effectiveness of the fractional HR model.

Chapter 4:

Financial Considerations

Implementing Fractional HR can be a game-changer for organizations looking to optimize their human resources functions while managing costs effectively. In this chapter, we will delve into the financial aspects of utilizing Fractional HR services, comparing it with traditional in-house HR teams, analyzing the return on investment (ROI), and providing guidance on budgeting for these services.

4.1 Cost Analysis of Fractional HR vs. In-House HR

When considering HR solutions, cost is a major factor. Businesses must weigh the financial implications of hiring an in-house HR team versus engaging Fractional HR services. This section breaks down the various costs associated with both models and explores the potential for cost savings.

Breakdown of Costs (Salary, Benefits, Overhead)

In-House HR Costs:

- **Salaries**: Hiring full-time HR professionals can be expensive. The average salary for an HR manager in the United States ranges from $70,000 to $120,000 annually, depending on experience and location. For senior HR positions, salaries can easily exceed $150,000.

- **Benefits**: Beyond salaries, employers must also cover benefits such as health insurance, retirement contributions (401(k) matching), paid time off, and other perks. These benefits typically add an additional 30-40% to the base salary.

- **Overhead Expenses**: In-house HR staff require office space, equipment (computers, phones), and software tools (HR management systems). The overhead associated with maintaining an HR department can be substantial, especially for small to mid-sized businesses.

- **Training and Development**: Investing in the continuous professional development of HR staff is necessary to keep them up-to-date with the latest regulations and best practices. These costs can include certifications, workshops, and conferences.

Fractional HR Costs:

- **Flexible Payment Structures**: Fractional HR services typically operate on flexible payment models, such as retainer fees, hourly rates, or project-based pricing. This allows businesses to pay only for the services they need when they need them.

- **No Additional Benefits**: One of the key financial advantages of Fractional HR is that you don't have to cover benefits like health insurance, retirement contributions, or paid time off, which reduces overall expenses.

- **Reduced Overhead**: Since Fractional HR professionals often work remotely or on a part-time basis, there are minimal overhead costs associated with office space, equipment, and utilities.

Example Cost Comparison:

- A mid-sized company with 100 employees might spend around $100,000 per year on a full-time HR Manager's salary and benefits. By contrast, a Fractional HR Manager could provide the same level of expertise and support for around $3,000-$5,000 per month, translating to an annual cost of $36,000-$60,000. This results in significant cost savings while still ensuring professional HR management.

Examples of Cost Savings with Fractional HR

- **Startup Scenario**: A tech startup in its growth phase needs HR support but cannot afford to hire a full-time HR Manager. By opting for a

Fractional HR solution, the company spends $2,000 per month on essential HR services like recruitment, compliance, and employee relations, saving over $80,000 annually compared to hiring a full-time employee.

- **Seasonal Businesses**: Companies with seasonal hiring needs, such as retail or hospitality businesses, can use Fractional HR services to handle peak hiring periods without the long-term commitment of a full-time HR staff. This flexibility results in cost savings and efficient resource allocation.

4.2 Return on Investment (ROI)

While cost savings are an important consideration, the true value of Fractional HR lies in its ability to drive business performance. Understanding the ROI of Fractional HR is essential for making informed decisions.

Measuring the Impact of Fractional HR on Business Performance

The ROI of Fractional HR can be measured by evaluating its impact on various HR metrics and overall business outcomes. Key areas where Fractional HR can deliver a strong ROI include:

- **Reduced Turnover**: Effective HR practices, such as improved onboarding and employee engagement strategies, can reduce turnover rates. Fractional HR professionals help create a positive work environment, leading to lower recruitment costs and increased employee retention.

- **Increased Productivity**: By streamlining HR processes, optimizing performance management systems, and implementing training programs, Fractional HR services can boost employee productivity and efficiency.

- **Compliance Risk Mitigation**: Fractional HR experts ensure that your company is compliant with labor laws and regulations, reducing the risk of costly legal issues and fines. This proactive approach to compliance can save businesses thousands of dollars in potential penalties.

- **Improved Recruitment Outcomes**: A Fractional HR Manager can enhance the quality of hires by implementing effective recruitment strategies, leading to better job performance and reduced hiring costs.

Case Studies Showing Financial Benefits

Case Study 1: A Small Manufacturing Company:

- Challenge: The company struggled with high employee turnover and compliance issues, leading to frequent fines and increased hiring costs.

- Solution: They engaged a Fractional HR expert to revamp their HR policies, improve the onboarding process, and implement employee engagement initiatives.

- Outcome: The company saw a 30% reduction in turnover and a significant decrease in compliance-related fines, resulting in annual savings of $50,000.

Case Study 2: A Growing Tech Firm:

- Challenge: The firm needed to scale its workforce quickly to meet project demands but lacked an efficient recruitment process.

- Solution: A Fractional HR consultant was brought in to optimize the recruitment pipeline, train hiring managers, and implement performance management systems.

- Outcome: The firm reduced its time-to-hire by 40%, increased new hire retention by 20%, and saved $60,000 in recruitment costs over one year.

4.3 Budgeting for Fractional HR Services

Before engaging Fractional HR services, it's essential to establish a budget that aligns with your organization's financial goals. This section provides practical tips for budgeting and forecasting HR costs.

Tips for Setting a Budget

- **Assess Your HR Needs**: Start by conducting a thorough assessment of your current HR processes and identifying areas where you need support. This can include compliance management, recruitment, performance management, or employee engagement.

- **Define Your Engagement Model**: Choose an engagement model that aligns with your budget and HR needs. For instance, a project-based model may be ideal for addressing specific HR challenges, while a retainer model offers ongoing support.

- **Consider the Scope of Services**: The cost of Fractional HR services varies depending on the scope of work. Determine whether you need comprehensive HR support or assistance with specific tasks like policy development, employee relations, or training.

- **Leverage Technology**: Utilizing HR software and tools can complement the services provided by Fractional HR professionals, reducing manual work and saving costs in the long run.

How to Forecast HR Costs with a Fractional Model

- **Analyze Historical Data**: Review your company's historical HR costs, including salaries, benefits, and recruitment expenses, to establish a baseline for your HR budget.

- **Estimate Service Fees**: Engage in discussions with potential Fractional HR providers to get a clear understanding of their pricing structures. This will help you estimate service fees and allocate funds accordingly.

- **Account for Growth**: If your business is in a growth phase, factor in the potential increase in HR needs, such as hiring, training, and compliance management. A scalable Fractional HR solution can accommodate these changes without significant cost increases.

- **Track and Adjust**: Implement a system for tracking HR expenses and regularly review your budget to ensure alignment with your financial goals. Adjust your budget as needed based on changes in business priorities or external factors.

Sample Budgeting Scenario:

- A retail business with 50 employees might allocate $4,000 per month for a Fractional HR service to handle compliance, recruitment, and employee engagement. Over a year, this would cost $48,000, compared to hiring a full-time HR Manager at $80,000 annually (including benefits), resulting in annual savings of $32,000.

Conclusion of Chapter 4

Investing in Fractional HR can yield significant financial benefits for businesses of all sizes, from cost savings to improved ROI through enhanced HR operations. By understanding the cost dynamics, measuring the impact of HR initiatives, and budgeting effectively, companies can leverage Fractional HR to optimize their human resources function and drive sustainable growth.

In the next chapter, we will explore **best practices for working with Fractional HR professionals**, including how to establish successful partnerships, set clear expectations, and maximize the value of your HR investment.

Chapter 5:

Choosing the Right Fractional HR Partner

Selecting the right Fractional HR partner is a critical decision that can significantly impact the success of your human resources strategy and, ultimately, your business. This chapter provides a comprehensive guide to choosing the ideal Fractional HR provider by examining key qualities, essential questions to ask during the selection process, and red flags to watch out for.

5.1 Key Qualities to Look for in a Fractional HR Provider

When searching for a Fractional HR partner, it's essential to identify a provider that aligns with your business needs and organizational culture. Here are some of the most important qualities to consider:

Relevant Industry Experience

- **Specialized Knowledge**: The HR landscape varies significantly across different industries. For example, the HR needs of a healthcare company differ from those of a tech startup. A Fractional HR partner with experience in your industry will have a deeper understanding of specific compliance requirements, hiring challenges, and industry trends. This specialized knowledge can translate into more effective HR strategies and solutions.

- **Proven Track Record**: Look for providers who have a history of success in your industry. Ask for case studies or references that demonstrate their expertise and results. For example, if your company is in manufacturing, find a partner who has successfully managed HR functions for other manufacturing businesses.

Strong Communication and Cultural Fit

- **Communication Skills**: An effective Fractional HR partner must possess excellent communication skills. They should be able to clearly articulate HR policies, provide timely updates, and foster open communication between management and employees. Strong communication ensures alignment with your company's goals and reduces misunderstandings.

- **Cultural Compatibility**: Your HR partner will play a significant role in shaping your company culture. It's essential to find someone who understands and aligns with your organizational values. For instance, if your company prioritizes employee engagement and work-life balance, your HR partner should share these values and help promote them.

Proven Track Record with Other Businesses

- **Client Testimonials and References**: A reliable Fractional HR partner should have a portfolio of satisfied clients. Request testimonials, case studies, or references to gain insight into their performance. Speaking directly with past clients can provide valuable information about their capabilities and work ethic.

- **Longevity of Relationships**: Look for providers who have established long-term relationships with their clients. Longevity often indicates a provider's reliability, trustworthiness, and ability to deliver consistent value over time.

5.2 Questions to Ask During the Selection Process

To ensure you're making the right choice, it's crucial to conduct a thorough evaluation of potential Fractional HR providers. Asking the right questions during the selection process can help you identify the best fit for your organization.

Sample Interview Questions for Potential HR Partners

1. **What industries have you worked in, and how do you tailor your HR services to meet industry-specific needs?**

   - This question assesses the provider's versatility and understanding of industry nuances.

2. **Can you share a success story where you helped a business overcome a significant HR challenge?**

   - Real-life examples demonstrate the provider's problem-solving skills and impact.

3. **What is your approach to handling sensitive employee issues, such as disciplinary actions or terminations?**

   - Understanding their approach to delicate matters will give you confidence in their professionalism and empathy.

4. **How do you stay updated with the latest HR laws and regulations?**

- This question tests their commitment to compliance and ongoing professional development.

5. **Can you describe the onboarding process for new clients?**

   - A well-structured onboarding process is a sign of a mature and efficient provider.

6. **What tools and technologies do you use to manage HR functions?**

   - Familiarity with the latest HR technology can improve efficiency and accuracy in HR processes.

7. **How do you measure the success of your HR strategies?**

   - This will help you understand their focus on results and their methods for tracking progress.

Evaluating Proposals and Service Agreements

- **Scope of Services**: Ensure that the provider's proposal clearly outlines the scope of services, including specific deliverables and timelines. This clarity helps prevent misunderstandings and ensures that your expectations align.

- **Pricing Structure**: Review the pricing model to ensure it fits within your budget. Some providers charge hourly rates, while others offer monthly retainers or project-based pricing. Make sure you understand the fee structure and any additional costs.

- **Service Level Agreements (SLAs)**: SLAs are crucial for setting clear expectations regarding response times, deliverables, and performance standards. Ensure that these agreements are detailed and aligned with your business requirements.

5.3 Red Flags to Watch Out For

While evaluating potential HR partners, it's important to be aware of warning signs that could indicate potential issues down the line.

Lack of Transparency in Pricing

- **Hidden Fees**: Be cautious of providers who are vague about their pricing or have a history of adding unexpected charges. Transparency in pricing is essential to avoid unpleasant surprises and ensure you can accurately budget for HR services.

- **Overly Low Rates**: If a provider's rates are significantly lower than the industry average, this could indicate a lack of experience or a reduced level of service quality. Remember, you often get what you pay for.

Overpromising Capabilities Without Evidence

- **Unrealistic Promises**: Beware of providers who guarantee immediate results or claim to have solutions for every problem. A reputable Fractional HR provider will be honest about their capabilities and limitations.

- **Lack of Case Studies or References**: If a provider is unable or unwilling to provide case studies, client references, or examples of their work, this could be a red flag. Established providers should have a portfolio of success stories to share.

Poor Communication Practices

- **Delayed Responses**: If a provider is slow to respond during the initial communication phase, this may indicate how they will handle future interactions. Effective communication is critical for a successful partnership.

- **Lack of Clarity**: Providers who fail to explain their services, processes, or pricing clearly may not be the best fit. Clear and transparent communication is essential for establishing trust.

Additional Red Flags to Consider:

- **High Turnover of HR Consultants**: Frequent changes in personnel can disrupt service quality and continuity.

- **Limited Service Offerings**: If a provider specializes in only one area of HR, they may not be able to address all your needs. Look for well-rounded expertise that covers the full spectrum of HR functions.

- **No Customization Options**: Every business is unique, so a one-size-fits-all approach may not be effective. Providers who do not offer customization may lack the flexibility to adapt to your specific requirements.

Conclusion of Chapter 5

Choosing the right Fractional HR partner is a critical decision that requires careful consideration of their experience, communication skills, and alignment with your business goals. By asking the right questions, evaluating proposals thoroughly, and being aware of potential red flags, you can find a partner who will add significant value to your HR operations and overall business success.

In the next chapter, we will discuss **best practices for managing a successful relationship with your Fractional HR partner**, including strategies for setting clear expectations, fostering collaboration, and measuring performance.

Chapter 6:

Real-Life Case Studies

In the world of Human Resources, the emergence of Fractional HR has proven to be a game-changer for many businesses, especially those looking for cost-effective and flexible solutions. This chapter explores real-life case studies that highlight the tangible benefits of Fractional HR, offering insights into how various organizations have successfully leveraged this model to address their HR needs. We'll look at examples from small businesses, industry-specific cases, and companies that overcame common HR challenges using a Fractional HR approach.

6.1 Small Business Success Stories

Fractional HR has become an invaluable asset for small businesses that often struggle with limited budgets and resources. Let's dive into a few success stories that demonstrate the positive impact of Fractional HR on small enterprises.

Case Study 1: A Boutique Marketing Agency's Growth Journey

The Challenge: A boutique marketing agency with 20 employees was experiencing rapid growth but lacked an in-house HR team to manage recruitment, compliance, and employee engagement. The agency's founders were handling HR tasks themselves, which diverted their focus from business development.

The Solution: The agency engaged a Fractional HR consultant on a retainer basis. The consultant focused on streamlining the recruitment process, implementing performance management systems, and improving employee engagement strategies.

Results:

- **Improved Recruitment**: The agency reduced its time-to-hire by 40% and increased the quality of new hires.

- **Enhanced Employee Satisfaction**: Employee engagement scores improved by 30% within six months.

- **Revenue Growth**: By delegating HR responsibilities to a professional, the founders were able to focus on business development, resulting in a 25% increase in revenue over a year.

Testimonial: *"Engaging a Fractional HR partner was the best decision we made. It allowed us to focus on what we do best while knowing our HR needs were in expert hands."* — Co-founder, Boutique Marketing Agency

Case Study 2: A Local Retail Store's Compliance Overhaul

The Challenge: A family-owned retail store with multiple locations faced challenges in keeping up with labor laws, especially as it expanded into new states. Compliance issues and employee grievances were becoming a significant concern.

The Solution: The store hired a Fractional HR consultant specializing in compliance and employee relations. The consultant audited the store's HR policies, updated the employee handbook, and conducted compliance training for store managers.

Results:

- **Reduced Legal Risks**: The store avoided potential fines by ensuring compliance with state-specific labor laws.

- **Better Employee Relations**: By addressing employee grievances promptly, the store saw a 50% decrease in turnover.

- **Cost Savings**: The store saved approximately $20,000 annually in potential legal fees.

Lesson Learned: For small businesses, Fractional HR can serve as a cost-effective solution to navigate the complexities of labor laws and compliance, especially when expanding to new markets.

6.2 Industry-Specific Case Studies

Different industries have unique HR challenges, and Fractional HR can offer tailored solutions to address these needs. Here, we explore how companies in the tech, healthcare, and retail sectors leveraged Fractional HR to their advantage.

Tech Industry: Scaling Up with Flexible HR Support

Case Study 3: A Growing Tech Startup's Talent Acquisition Strategy

The Challenge: A tech startup specializing in AI software was experiencing a surge in demand. The company needed to scale up its team quickly but didn't have the resources to hire a full-time HR team.

The Solution: The startup engaged a Fractional HR manager with experience in tech recruitment. The HR manager helped create job descriptions, streamlined the interview process, and set up an employee referral program.

Results:

- **Faster Hiring**: The company hired 10 developers and engineers within three months, reducing time-to-hire by 50%.

- **Cost Efficiency**: The startup saved $50,000 in recruitment agency fees by handling the process in-house with the support of their Fractional HR manager.

- **Enhanced Employer Branding**: The new onboarding process improved employee satisfaction, helping the company attract top talent.

Healthcare Industry: Compliance and Employee Retention

Case Study 4: A Regional Healthcare Provider's Compliance Strategy

The Challenge: A regional healthcare provider with 100 employees faced challenges in maintaining compliance with ever-changing healthcare regulations. The internal HR team was overwhelmed with managing compliance audits, staff training, and employee performance reviews.

The Solution: The provider brought in a Fractional HR consultant specializing in healthcare compliance. The consultant developed a comprehensive compliance program, conducted regular audits, and implemented a training schedule for staff.

Results:

- **Improved Compliance**: The healthcare provider passed its next audit with flying colors, avoiding penalties.

- **Increased Staff Retention**: By offering ongoing training and development, employee turnover reduced by 20%.

- **Boosted Morale**: Employees appreciated the focus on professional development, leading to higher engagement scores.

Retail Industry: Enhancing Employee Engagement

Case Study 5: A Fashion Retailer's Engagement Initiative

The Challenge: A mid-sized fashion retailer struggled with high turnover, particularly among its sales associates. Exit interviews revealed low employee engagement and lack of recognition as key issues.

The Solution: The retailer hired a Fractional HR partner to develop an employee engagement program. This included implementing regular feedback sessions, introducing a rewards program, and organizing team-building activities.

Results:

- **Lower Turnover**: The retailer saw a 35% reduction in turnover rates within six months.

- **Higher Sales**: Engaged employees contributed to a 15% increase in store sales during the same period.

- **Positive Workplace Culture**: The retailer developed a reputation as a great place to work, attracting better talent.

6.3 Overcoming Common Challenges with Fractional HR

Fractional HR not only offers flexibility but also helps businesses overcome common HR challenges that may otherwise hinder growth. Let's explore how different organizations used Fractional HR to address their specific pain points.

Challenge 1: Managing Remote Teams

Case Study 6: A Remote SaaS Company's Performance Management Overhaul

The Challenge: A SaaS company with a fully remote workforce struggled with managing performance across different time zones and cultures. The lack of a structured performance review system led to inconsistencies in employee evaluations.

The Solution: The company brought in a Fractional HR consultant to design a performance management system tailored to remote teams. The system included regular check-ins, 360-degree feedback, and goal-setting workshops.

Results:

- **Increased Productivity**: The structured approach led to a 20% increase in employee productivity.

- **Better Alignment**: Employees had clearer performance expectations, which aligned with company goals.

- **Stronger Team Collaboration**: Regular feedback sessions improved communication among remote team members.

Challenge 2: Scaling Operations During Rapid Growth

Case Study 7: An E-commerce Startup's HR Expansion Plan

The Challenge: An e-commerce startup was scaling rapidly but faced challenges in expanding its HR operations to support the growing workforce. The internal HR team was overwhelmed with recruitment, onboarding, and compliance tasks.

The Solution: The startup engaged a Fractional HR manager who specialized in high-growth environments. The HR manager helped streamline HR processes, set up automated systems, and trained the internal HR team.

Results:

- **Operational Efficiency**: The company reduced the time spent on manual HR tasks by 40%.

- **Scalable HR Framework**: The startup implemented scalable HR systems that could grow with the company.

- **Cost Savings**: By optimizing HR processes, the company saved $30,000 annually on HR-related costs.

Challenge 3: Improving Employee Satisfaction

Case Study 8: A Professional Services Firm's Employee Satisfaction Initiative

The Challenge: A professional services firm with 50 employees had low morale and high turnover, primarily due to a lack of clear career progression and employee recognition.

The Solution: The firm hired a Fractional HR consultant to conduct employee surveys, develop career paths, and implement a recognition program.

Results:

- **Increased Retention**: The firm reduced turnover by 25% within a year.

- **Employee Satisfaction**: Satisfaction scores improved significantly, leading to better client service.

- **Positive Reputation**: The firm became known for its employee-centric culture, attracting top talent in the industry.

Conclusion of Chapter 6

These real-life case studies demonstrate the versatility and effectiveness of Fractional HR across various industries and business sizes. Whether addressing compliance issues, improving employee engagement, or supporting rapid growth, Fractional HR can provide tailored solutions that deliver measurable results. By leveraging the expertise of seasoned HR professionals on a flexible basis, businesses can overcome challenges and achieve sustainable growth.

In the next chapter, we will explore **best practices for integrating Fractional HR into your existing HR strategy,** including tips for fostering collaboration between internal teams and external HR partners.

Chapter 7:

Common Myths & Misconceptions About Fractional HR

Despite the growing popularity of Fractional HR, several myths and misconceptions can prevent businesses from fully embracing this innovative approach to human resources. In this chapter, we'll debunk some of the most common myths surrounding Fractional HR, shedding light on how it can benefit businesses of all sizes and dispelling concerns about commitment, control, and effectiveness.

7.1 Myth: Fractional HR Is Only for Small Businesses

One of the most pervasive myths about Fractional HR is that it's only suitable for small businesses with limited budgets. This misconception can prevent medium and large enterprises from leveraging the flexibility and expertise that Fractional HR offers. Let's explore why this myth is inaccurate and how companies of all sizes can benefit from a Fractional HR approach.

Debunking the Myth

While it's true that many small businesses have turned to Fractional HR as a cost-effective solution for managing their HR needs, the benefits extend far beyond the small business segment. Medium and large organizations can also take advantage of Fractional HR for several reasons:

1. **Scaling HR Capabilities**:

   - As companies grow, their HR needs become more complex. Fractional HR provides a scalable solution, allowing organizations to access specialized HR skills without committing to full-time hires.

- For example, a large tech company expanding into new markets may require expertise in international labor laws, compliance, and cultural differences. A Fractional HR specialist with international experience can offer targeted support.

2. **Cost Efficiency:**

- Large organizations may not always require full-time HR professionals for specific projects or temporary needs. Fractional HR allows these businesses to access senior HR expertise on an as-needed basis, saving on salaries, benefits, and overhead costs.
- Consider a manufacturing company undergoing a restructuring process. Instead of hiring a full-time change management consultant, they could bring in a Fractional HR expert to guide the transition, saving both time and money.

3. **Filling Temporary Gaps:**

- Medium and large businesses often face temporary HR staffing gaps due to maternity leave, long-term sick leave, or sudden departures. Fractional HR professionals can step in to cover these gaps seamlessly, ensuring continuity in HR operations.

- A healthcare organization, for instance, may need interim HR support during a leadership transition. A Fractional HR manager can maintain stability until a permanent replacement is found.

Real-World Example

A Fortune 500 company faced challenges in diversity, equity, and inclusion (DEI) initiatives. Instead of hiring a full-time DEI officer, they engaged a Fractional HR consultant with extensive experience in DEI programs. The consultant developed a comprehensive strategy, trained the internal HR team, and set up metrics to track progress, all within six months. The company not only met its DEI goals but also saved significant costs by using a Fractional HR approach.

7.2 Myth: Fractional HR Lacks Commitment

Another common misconception is that Fractional HR professionals lack the commitment of full-time employees, leading to concerns about their dedication, availability, and integration into the company culture. This myth can cause hesitation among businesses considering a Fractional HR model.

Addressing the Concerns

Contrary to the belief that Fractional HR professionals are less committed, many bring a high level of dedication, driven by their desire to deliver results and build lasting client relationships. Here's why Fractional HR professionals are often just as, if not more, committed than in-house HR staff:

1. **Focus on Deliverables:**

   - Fractional HR professionals are typically results-driven. They are hired to achieve specific goals and are motivated to meet or exceed expectations to secure repeat business and referrals.
   - A Fractional HR consultant hired to improve employee engagement is likely to invest significant effort into developing

surveys, analyzing feedback, and implementing actionable strategies, knowing that their performance is directly tied to the client's satisfaction.

2. **Specialized Expertise:**

- Fractional HR professionals often have years of experience across various industries and bring specialized skills to the table. They are passionate about their work and are eager to apply their expertise to new challenges.
- For instance, a Fractional HR expert in compliance is dedicated to keeping up with the latest labor laws and regulations, ensuring that the client remains compliant and avoids costly legal issues.

3. **Flexibility and Adaptability:**

- Fractional HR professionals are accustomed to working with different organizations, which makes them highly adaptable. They are skilled at quickly integrating into new environments, understanding company cultures, and building rapport with teams.

- A Fractional HR manager brought in for a culture transformation project can leverage their adaptability to gain trust from employees and leadership alike, driving meaningful change.

Real-World Example

A mid-sized financial services firm was concerned about the commitment level of a Fractional HR partner they considered hiring to revamp their performance management system. However, after engaging the Fractional HR professional, they found that her commitment to delivering a robust and customized solution far exceeded their expectations. The consultant worked closely with senior leaders, conducted thorough assessments, and implemented a new system that boosted productivity by 20%.

7.3 Myth: Outsourcing HR Means Losing Control

One of the biggest fears organizations have when considering Fractional HR is the perception that outsourcing HR functions means losing control over their processes, policies, and company culture. This misconception can lead businesses to resist adopting Fractional HR solutions, even when it could be in their best interest.

How Fractional HR Provides Control with Flexibility

Outsourcing HR doesn't equate to relinquishing control. In fact, Fractional HR offers a balanced approach where businesses can maintain oversight while benefiting from external expertise. Here's how:

1. **Customized Service Agreements:**

   - Fractional HR services are tailored to meet the specific needs of the organization. Companies can outline the scope of work, set clear deliverables, and define expectations upfront, ensuring they remain in control of the process.
   - For example, a company that wants to outsource only its recruitment efforts can work with a Fractional HR partner to focus exclusively on sourcing, interviewing, and hiring, while retaining control over the final hiring decisions.

2. **Enhanced Control Through Expertise:**

- Fractional HR professionals often bring best practices and proven methodologies to the table. By leveraging their expertise, companies can gain better control over HR processes, improve efficiency, and reduce risks.
- An organization struggling with high turnover can collaborate with a Fractional HR expert to diagnose the root causes and implement retention strategies, thus gaining control over employee satisfaction and reducing churn.

3. **Transparent Reporting and Communication**:

- Effective Fractional HR partners prioritize transparency and regular communication. They provide detailed reports, progress updates, and data-driven insights, allowing businesses to stay informed and make strategic decisions.
- A retail chain working with a Fractional HR consultant on compliance issues can receive monthly compliance reports, enabling them to monitor the status of audits, policy updates, and training programs.

Real-World Example

A nonprofit organization was hesitant to outsource its HR functions due to concerns about losing control over its mission-driven culture. However, after partnering with a Fractional HR consultant, they found that the consultant was able to align HR practices with the organization's values. By introducing employee engagement initiatives that resonated with their mission, the consultant not only preserved the culture but also enhanced it.

Conclusion of Chapter 7

The myths surrounding Fractional HR can be significant barriers to adopting this flexible, cost-effective model. However, as we've explored, these misconceptions often stem from misunderstandings about how Fractional HR works.

- **Fractional HR is not just for small businesses**; it provides scalable, expert solutions for organizations of all sizes, from startups to established enterprises.

- **Commitment is not an issue** with Fractional HR professionals, who are often highly dedicated to delivering value and achieving client satisfaction.

- **Outsourcing HR does not mean losing control**; rather, it offers businesses a way to enhance their HR capabilities while maintaining oversight and flexibility.

As more organizations recognize the benefits of Fractional HR, it's clear that this model can drive growth, reduce costs, and improve HR outcomes. By debunking these myths, businesses can make informed decisions about whether Fractional HR is the right fit for their needs.

In the next chapter, we will explore **best practices for integrating Fractional HR into your existing HR strategy**, focusing on how to maximize the value of this partnership for long-term success.

Chapter 8:

The Future of Fractional HR

The world of human resources is undergoing a profound transformation, driven by technological advancements, shifting workforce expectations, and the demand for more flexible business solutions. As organizations navigate the complexities of modern HR, the Fractional HR model has emerged as a game-changer, offering businesses the ability to scale their HR functions in a cost-effective and agile manner. In this chapter, we will explore the trends shaping the HR industry, predictions for the future of Fractional HR, and practical steps businesses can take to prepare for the evolving HR landscape.

8.1 Trends Shaping the HR Industry

The HR industry is constantly evolving, with new trends emerging that significantly impact how organizations manage their workforce. Fractional HR, which offers on-demand expertise without the commitment of full-time staff, is uniquely positioned to leverage these trends. Let's delve into some of the key trends driving the growth of Fractional HR.

The Rise of Remote Work and Its Impact on HR Functions

The COVID-19 pandemic accelerated the adoption of remote work, leading to a fundamental shift in how businesses operate. Even as the world returns to normalcy, remote and hybrid work models have become the norm rather than the exception.

1. **Decentralized Workforce Management**:
   - HR teams are now responsible for managing a distributed workforce, which requires new strategies for employee

engagement, performance management, and communication. Fractional HR professionals, who are often accustomed to remote work themselves, can provide the expertise needed to adapt HR practices for remote teams.

- For instance, a Fractional HR specialist can help develop remote onboarding processes, virtual team-building activities, and strategies for maintaining a strong company culture in a virtual environment.

2. **Focus on Employee Well-being**:

- With remote work blurring the lines between personal and professional life, employee well-being has become a top priority. Fractional HR experts can guide businesses in implementing mental health initiatives, flexible work policies, and wellness programs that support a healthier work-life balance.

The Role of Technology in Enabling Fractional HR Services

The digital transformation of HR has paved the way for Fractional HR services to thrive. Technology not only enables HR professionals to work remotely but also streamlines HR processes, making it easier for businesses to access the expertise they need.

HR Tech Tools and Automation:

The use of HR software, such as Applicant Tracking Systems (ATS), Human Resource Management Systems (HRMS), and Learning Management Systems (LMS), allows Fractional HR professionals to efficiently manage recruitment, performance reviews, and employee training from anywhere in the world.

Automation tools help Fractional HR consultants handle repetitive tasks, such as payroll processing, benefits administration, and compliance reporting, freeing up time for strategic HR initiatives.

Data-Driven Decision Making:

Access to real-time data and analytics has empowered HR professionals to make more informed decisions. Fractional HR providers use data analytics to assess employee engagement, turnover rates, and performance metrics, allowing businesses to address issues proactively.

Growing Demand for Flexible and Agile HR Solutions

In today's dynamic business environment, organizations are looking for ways to remain agile and responsive to change. The demand for flexible HR solutions is on the rise, and Fractional HR offers a model that aligns perfectly with this need.

Scalability and Flexibility:

Fractional HR allows businesses to scale their HR operations up or down based on demand, making it an ideal solution for startups, seasonal businesses, or organizations experiencing rapid growth. Companies can access specialized HR skills for short-term projects, such as mergers and acquisitions or organizational restructuring, without the need for long-term commitments.

Cost-Effectiveness:

By engaging Fractional HR services, companies can access top-tier HR talent without incurring the costs associated with full-time employees, such as salaries, benefits, and overhead expenses. This cost-efficiency is particularly appealing to organizations looking to optimize their HR budgets.

8.2 Predictions for the Future

The Fractional HR model is set to evolve in response to ongoing changes in the business landscape. Here are some predictions for how this model will adapt to meet future challenges and opportunities.

How the Fractional HR Model Will Evolve

Increased Specialization:

As the demand for niche HR expertise grows, we are likely to see a rise in highly specialized Fractional HR providers. These experts will offer deep knowledge in areas such as diversity, equity, and inclusion (DEI), talent acquisition for specific industries, or global HR compliance.

For example, companies expanding into new international markets may seek Fractional HR consultants with experience in global talent management and international labor laws.

Integration with AI and Machine Learning:

Artificial Intelligence (AI) and Machine Learning (ML) are transforming the HR industry, from AI-driven recruitment platforms to predictive analytics for employee retention. Fractional HR providers who embrace these technologies will be better positioned to offer data-driven insights and automated solutions to their clients.

Growth of Fractional HR Networks and Marketplaces:

As the gig economy continues to expand, we can expect the emergence of online platforms and marketplaces that connect businesses with vetted Fractional HR professionals. These platforms will make it easier for companies to find, hire, and manage HR talent on a fractional basis.

Potential Challenges and Opportunities in the Market

Challenges:

Talent Shortages: As the demand for Fractional HR professionals grows, there may be a shortage of qualified candidates, especially those with specialized skills.

Maintaining Consistency: Companies may face challenges in maintaining consistency in HR practices when using multiple Fractional HR providers across different regions or projects.

Opportunities:

Expansion into New Markets: The shift towards remote work has opened up global talent pools, allowing Fractional HR providers to serve clients across different geographies.

Increased Demand for DEI Initiatives: As organizations prioritize diversity, equity, and inclusion, there will be a growing demand for

Fractional HR experts who can lead DEI initiatives and foster inclusive workplace cultures.

8.3 Preparing Your Business for the Future

As the HR landscape continues to evolve, organizations need to be proactive in adapting to these changes. Here are some strategies to help your business stay ahead of the curve and maximize the benefits of Fractional HR.

Steps to Adapt to Changing HR Landscapes

Conduct an HR Needs Assessment:

Start by evaluating your current HR capabilities and identifying gaps that could be filled by Fractional HR professionals. Consider areas such as compliance, talent acquisition, employee engagement, and training.

For example, if your organization is planning to expand rapidly, you may need additional support in recruitment and onboarding. A Fractional HR consultant with experience in high-growth environments can help streamline these processes.

Leverage Technology for HR Operations:

Invest in HR technology that supports remote collaboration, data analysis, and automation. This will not only enhance the efficiency of your HR team but also enable seamless integration with Fractional HR providers.

Implementing tools like cloud-based HR systems, virtual meeting platforms, and digital onboarding solutions can make it easier to collaborate with Fractional HR professionals.

Embrace a Culture of Continuous Learning and Development:

The future of HR will require a focus on continuous learning to keep up with changing regulations, technology, and best practices. Encourage your HR team and leadership to participate in ongoing training and development programs.

Fractional HR experts can also support your organization's learning initiatives by providing specialized training sessions, workshops, and coaching.

The Role of Continuous Learning and Development in HR

Upskilling and Reskilling:

As job roles evolve, there is a growing need for upskilling and reskilling initiatives. Fractional HR professionals can help design and implement training programs that address skill gaps and prepare your workforce for future challenges.

For instance, a Fractional HR consultant can develop a leadership development program that equips managers with the skills needed to lead remote teams effectively.

Staying Updated on Compliance and Legal Changes:

Labor laws and regulations are constantly changing, and businesses need to stay compliant to avoid penalties. Fractional HR providers can offer expertise in navigating these changes, ensuring that your policies and practices remain up to date.

Fostering Innovation and Agility:

Continuous learning fosters a culture of innovation, which is essential in a rapidly changing business environment. By partnering with Fractional HR experts, businesses can access fresh perspectives and innovative HR solutions that drive growth and competitiveness.

Conclusion of Chapter 8

The future of HR is evolving rapidly, with technology, remote work, and the demand for flexibility driving significant changes. Fractional HR is uniquely positioned to meet these challenges, offering businesses the ability to scale HR functions, access specialized expertise, and remain agile in an ever-changing landscape.

Trends such as remote work and HR technology are reshaping how organizations manage their workforce, creating new opportunities for Fractional HR providers.

Predictions for the future of Fractional HR indicate a shift towards increased specialization, integration with AI, and the growth of online HR marketplaces.

To prepare for the future, businesses should assess their HR needs, invest in technology, and embrace a culture of continuous learning and innovation.

By staying ahead of these trends and leveraging the benefits of Fractional HR, organizations can enhance their HR capabilities, drive business performance, and thrive in a competitive market.

Conclusion

As businesses face the ever-evolving challenges of managing their workforce, Fractional HR has emerged as a transformative solution, offering an innovative way to meet HR needs while maintaining flexibility and cost-effectiveness. In this book, we have explored the many facets of Fractional HR—its benefits, implementation strategies, and the long-term value it can bring to organizations of all sizes. To conclude, let's recap the key takeaways, discuss next steps for getting started with Fractional HR, and offer a call to action for businesses to assess their HR needs.

Recap of Key Takeaways

Throughout this book, we have seen how Fractional HR offers businesses a range of benefits, particularly for companies seeking flexible, cost-efficient, and expert-driven HR support. Let's recap the most important points:

1. The Benefits of Fractional HR:

Cost-Effective Solution: Fractional HR allows businesses to access high-level HR expertise without the financial burden of hiring a full-time HR team. By paying only for the services you need, you can reduce overhead costs while still receiving top-notch HR management.

- **Flexibility and Scalability:** With Fractional HR, you can scale your HR functions based on your needs, whether it's for a one-off project, seasonal support, or ongoing assistance. This flexibility ensures that your business can adapt to changing needs without the commitment of a full-time employee.

- **Access to Expertise:** Fractional HR providers often bring specialized skills and industry experience, enabling them to address specific challenges and provide strategic guidance on issues such as talent acquisition, compliance, employee engagement, and organizational development.

- **Improved Business Performance:** By partnering with Fractional HR professionals, businesses can streamline HR operations, implement better employee practices, and create a stronger company culture—

ultimately leading to improved overall performance and growth.

- **Enhancing Strategic Focus:** With Fractional HR handling day-to-day HR tasks, business leaders can focus on driving strategic initiatives. This delegation of responsibility allows for greater focus on business growth, innovation, and customer satisfaction.

2. Key Strategies for Implementing Fractional HR:

- **Assess Your Needs:** To successfully implement Fractional HR, start by evaluating your current HR requirements. Determine which areas of HR require support, such as recruitment, compliance, employee training, or organizational restructuring.

- **Choose the Right Partner:** As discussed in Chapter 5, selecting the right Fractional HR provider is critical. Look for candidates with relevant industry experience, strong communication skills, and a proven track record of success. Conduct interviews, ask detailed questions, and ensure that the provider understands your company culture and objectives.

- **Integrate Fractional HR into Your Existing Structure:** Fractional HR professionals should be seen as an extension of your team. Develop clear communication channels, establish expectations, and define goals to ensure seamless integration. Effective collaboration between in-house teams and external HR partners will help you maximize the value of the partnership.

- **Monitor and Measure Impact:** Regularly assess the impact of Fractional HR services on your business. Evaluate metrics such as employee satisfaction, retention rates, recruitment success, and compliance levels. Using these insights will help you make adjustments to your strategy and further optimize the benefits of Fractional HR.

3. The Value of Fractional HR in the Modern Business Landscape:

As the HR landscape continues to evolve with advancements in technology, remote work, and growing demands for flexible solutions,

Fractional HR provides a solution that aligns with the future of work. Businesses can achieve a competitive advantage by accessing specialized HR expertise, fostering a healthy organizational culture, and maintaining compliance with shifting regulations—all while managing costs effectively.

The future of HR is flexible, agile, and technology-driven, and Fractional HR is poised to play a major role in this evolution. As more companies turn to remote, hybrid, and flexible work models, the need for strategic HR solutions that can adapt to these changes will continue to rise.

Next Steps

Now that you have a comprehensive understanding of the benefits and implementation strategies of Fractional HR, it's time to take action. Here are the steps you can follow to get started with Fractional HR:

How to Get Started with Fractional HR:

Evaluate Your HR Needs:

Take the time to conduct a thorough HR audit. Identify gaps in your current HR functions and areas where you need support. Do you need assistance with compliance, recruitment, training, or improving employee engagement? Understanding where Fractional HR can add value is crucial for finding the right provider.

Create a Clear HR Strategy:

Define your goals and expectations for HR. Whether you're looking for short-term support or a long-term strategic partner, creating a clear plan will help you communicate your needs effectively and ensure the right fit with a Fractional HR provider.

Research and Select a Fractional HR Provider:

Once you've assessed your needs, start researching potential Fractional HR partners. Look for providers who specialize in your industry or specific HR needs. Read reviews, ask for testimonials, and meet with candidates to assess their expertise and compatibility with your organization.

Establish an Agreement:

Draft a service agreement that outlines the scope of work, compensation, expectations, timelines, and communication protocols. Having a clear and formal agreement will ensure a successful partnership and prevent misunderstandings down the line.

Integrate HR into Your Workflow:

Work with your Fractional HR provider to integrate them into your business. Set up regular check-ins, establish communication channels, and ensure they have the tools they need to perform their role effectively.

Track Progress and Make Adjustments:

After a few months of working with Fractional HR, assess the impact on your business. Are you meeting your HR goals? Are employees more satisfied, and are you seeing improvements in recruitment and retention? Use these insights to make any necessary adjustments.

Resources for Further Learning:

HR Associations and Networks: Joining professional HR organizations can provide you with ongoing education and networking opportunities. Consider organizations like the Society for Human Resource Management (SHRM) or the HR Certification Institute (HRCI).

HR Technology Tools: Explore tools that can help automate and streamline your HR processes. Platforms such as BambooHR, Workday, and ADP offer comprehensive HR solutions that can complement your Fractional HR services.

Webinars and Conferences: Stay up to date with the latest HR trends by attending webinars, virtual conferences, and HR events. Many of these events feature thought leaders in the HR field and offer valuable insights into best practices, technology, and evolving workforce trends.

Books and Articles on HR Best Practices: Expand your knowledge with books on leadership, HR strategy, employee engagement, and compliance. Look for resources that offer practical, actionable advice to help you improve HR practices within your organization.

Call to Action

Are you ready to evaluate your current HR needs and explore the benefits of Fractional HR? Whether you are a small business looking for expert HR support or a growing company needing flexible, cost-effective HR solutions, now is the time to consider this transformative model.

To help you get started, we offer a **free consultation** to assess your unique HR requirements and provide recommendations tailored to your business. At Crystal Coast HR Our experts can guide you through the process of selecting the right Fractional HR provider and setting up a plan for success.

Additionally, **download our free resource**: "Fractional HR Checklist for Success," which provides actionable steps and helpful tips to get the most out of your Fractional HR partnership.

Take control of your HR strategy today and position your business for long-term success with Fractional HR. Contact us to schedule your free consultation or download our guide now!

Final Thought:

The future of HR is here, and Fractional HR is leading the way. By embracing this flexible, cost-effective approach, businesses can navigate the complexities of the modern workforce and create a thriving, engaged, and compliant workforce. Don't wait to get started—take the first step toward transforming your HR strategy today.

Appendix

In this section, we provide additional resources to help business owners and HR professionals better understand the concepts discussed in this eBook. The following sections include a **Glossary of HR Terms** to clarify important terminology, **Resources & Tools** for further learning and practical implementation, and a **Frequently Asked Questions (FAQ)** section to address common concerns about Fractional HR.

Glossary of HR Terms

Understanding HR terminology is essential for navigating the complexities of Human Resources management, especially when exploring Fractional HR. Here's a glossary of key HR-related terms to help clarify the language used throughout the eBook:

- **Applicant Tracking System (ATS):** A software application used by HR departments to manage the recruitment process, including the collection and processing of resumes, tracking job candidates, and automating certain aspects of hiring.

- **Compensation & Benefits:** Refers to the combination of salary or wages, benefits (such as healthcare, retirement plans, etc.), and other perks provided to employees in exchange for their work.

- **Employee Engagement:** A measure of how emotionally invested employees are in their work, and how committed they are to the organization's goals. High employee engagement typically leads to improved productivity, retention, and morale.

- **Employee Retention:** The ability of an organization to keep its employees over time. High retention rates are often seen as a sign of a healthy organizational culture and effective leadership.

- **HR Audit:** A comprehensive review of a company's HR policies, procedures, and practices to ensure compliance with legal standards and internal best practices. An HR audit may be conducted periodically to identify areas for improvement.

- **Job Descriptions:** Documents that clearly define the responsibilities, qualifications, and expectations for a specific role within an organization. They are crucial for recruitment and setting employee performance standards.

- **Key Performance Indicators (KPIs):** Metrics used to measure the performance of employees, departments, or organizations. KPIs are often tied to organizational goals and are used to assess success or identify areas for improvement.

- **Onboarding:** The process of integrating new employees into the organization. This includes the completion of necessary paperwork, introductions to company culture, training, and support during the initial period of employment.

- **Outsourcing:** The practice of contracting external parties to handle certain business functions or processes, such as HR, rather than maintaining those functions in-house. Fractional HR is an example of outsourcing HR services.

- **Performance Management:** A set of processes aimed at monitoring and improving employee performance. This includes regular feedback, goal setting, and performance reviews to help employees align with organizational objectives.

- **Recruitment:** The process of identifying, attracting, and selecting qualified candidates to fill job openings. Effective recruitment strategies are essential to building a strong workforce.

- **Succession Planning:** A process to identify and develop internal employees who can fill key leadership roles in the future. It ensures the company is prepared for leadership transitions.

- **Workforce Planning:** The process of analyzing an organization's current and future staffing needs and developing strategies to meet those needs. This includes identifying skill gaps, creating talent pipelines, and ensuring that the right people are in the right roles.

- **Workplace Diversity & Inclusion:** The practice of creating a workforce that reflects a variety of backgrounds, perspectives, and experiences, and fostering an inclusive environment where all employees feel valued and respected.

Resources & Tools

To help you deepen your knowledge and improve your HR practices, we've compiled a list of recommended resources and tools that are valuable for anyone exploring HR management and Fractional HR services.

Books on HR Management:

"The New HR Leader's First 100 Days" by Alan Collins

A practical guide for HR professionals who are stepping into leadership roles, with a focus on creating impact in the first few months.

"Drive: The Surprising Truth About What Motivates Us" by Daniel H. Pink

An essential read for anyone interested in employee motivation and how to create a workplace that encourages engagement and high performance.

"First Break All the Rules: What the World's Greatest Managers Do Differently" by Marcus Buckingham and Curt Coffman

This book provides insights into how the best managers create an environment that fosters employee success and growth.

"Work Rules!" by Laszlo Bock

Former Google HR leader Laszlo Bock offers a behind-the-scenes look at the innovative HR practices that helped Google become one of the best places to work.

Articles & Journals:

Harvard Business Review (HBR)

A leading source of research-based articles on leadership, HR management, employee engagement, and organizational strategy.

SHRM (Society for Human Resource Management)

The world's largest HR membership organization provides access to research, best practices, templates, and educational resources on various HR topics.

McKinsey & Company Insights on HR and Leadership

McKinsey's research and case studies offer valuable insights on organizational behavior, HR trends, and leadership strategies.

Online Courses:

EBL Training – HR for People Managers Specialization

An excellent series of courses that cover everything from recruitment to performance management. This is perfect for managers or business owners who want to improve their HR knowledge.

LinkedIn Learning – HR Essentials

A collection of bite-sized courses on essential HR topics, including hiring strategies, employee development, and compliance.

Udemy – Human Resource Management (HRM) Certification

Offers a comprehensive look at HR practices, from the basics of recruitment to advanced management strategies.

HR Templates:

- **Employee Handbook Template:** A comprehensive document that outlines your company's policies, values, and expectations, ensuring consistency across the organization.

- **Job Description Template:** A customizable template to help you clearly define the responsibilities, qualifications, and skills required for each role.

- **Performance Review Template:** This template provides a structured format for evaluating employee performance, including goal-setting and feedback sections.

- **Onboarding Checklist:** A checklist to ensure that new hires complete all necessary steps to begin their employment, including documentation, training, and introductions.

- **Exit Interview Template:** A structured format for conducting exit interviews to gain insights into the reasons why employees leave, which can help improve retention strategies.

HR Tools:

1. **BambooHR:** An all-in-one HR software designed for small to medium-sized businesses. BambooHR helps you track employee data, manage benefits, and automate time-off requests.

2. **Workday:** An enterprise-level HR tool offering a comprehensive suite of applications for managing HR processes, including payroll, performance, recruitment, and talent management.

3. **Gusto:** A simple payroll, benefits, and HR tool ideal for small businesses. Gusto simplifies hiring, managing benefits, and ensuring compliance with labor laws.

4. **Zenefits:** A platform that helps companies manage HR functions like onboarding, benefits administration, and time off tracking—all in one place.

Frequently Asked Questions (FAQ)

In this section, we address some common questions that business owners and managers often have when considering Fractional HR services.

1. What exactly is Fractional HR?

Answer:
Fractional HR refers to outsourcing specific HR functions or having a part-time HR professional handle your company's HR needs. Unlike traditional full-time HR staff, Fractional HR allows businesses to access specialized HR expertise as needed, without the cost of a full-time hire. It's particularly beneficial for small to mid-sized businesses looking to scale operations without expanding their internal HR teams.

2. How does Fractional HR benefit small businesses?

Answer:
Small businesses often struggle to afford a full-time HR team. Fractional HR allows these businesses to tap into high-level HR expertise for

a fraction of the cost. It provides them with the tools to handle recruitment, compliance, performance management, and other critical HR functions, all while saving on overhead costs like salaries, benefits, and office space.

3. Is Fractional HR a temporary solution, or can it be long-term?

Answer:

Fractional HR can be both a temporary and long-term solution, depending on your business's needs. Some businesses use Fractional HR for short-term projects like recruiting or compliance audits, while others build long-term partnerships for ongoing HR support. It's a flexible model that can evolve with your company's growth.

4. How do I know if Fractional HR is the right fit for my business?

Answer:

To determine if Fractional HR is the right choice for your business, assess your HR needs. If you find that you need specialized HR services but don't have the resources to hire a full-time team, Fractional HR may be an ideal solution. If your company is growing and the demands on your

HR functions are increasing, Fractional HR can help manage this transition effectively.

5. How do I ensure a smooth transition when implementing Fractional HR?

Answer:
A smooth transition requires clear communication and integration. Start by setting clear expectations with your Fractional HR provider, including goals, timelines, and roles. Ensure there's a structured process for collaboration between the external HR team and your in-house employees. Regular check-ins and performance reviews will also help ensure that the partnership is working effectively.

Conclusion

By leveraging Fractional HR, businesses can access expert HR services without the cost and commitment of a full-time hire. Whether you're a small business owner looking to streamline HR functions or a growing company seeking flexible solutions, Fractional HR offers a valuable way to manage your workforce efficiently. With the right resources, tools, and knowledge, you can build an effective HR strategy that fosters growth, compliance, and employee satisfaction.

Contact Information:

Crystal Coast HR

(252) 668-1640

Mike@CrystalCoastHR.com